Moderately

it's no fun _____

drink - ing _____ beer in the back ___ seat, _____

___ all a - lone just ain't ___

___ too ___ neat, _____ at the

pas - sion pit want - ing _____ you. _____

And when the in - ter - mis - sion _____ elf moves the

clock's ___ hands, _ while he's eat - ing _____ ev - 'ry -

thing sold at the stand, _____ when there's

HAL•LEONARD

Pro Vocal®
BETTER THAN KARAOKE!

FOR MALE SINGERS

BROADWAY SONGS

CONTENTS

Cover photo by Anne Clausen

ISBN 0-634-06303-0

HAL•LEONARD®
CORPORATION
7777 W. BLUEMOUND RD. P.O. BOX 13819 MILWAUKEE, WI 53213

Visit Hal Leonard Online at
www.halleonard.com

Alone at the Drive-In Movie

from GREASE

Lyric and Music by WARREN CASEY and JIM JACOBS

Any Dream Will Do

from JOSEPH AND THE AMAZING TECHNICOLOR DREAMCOAT

Music by ANDREW LLOYD WEBBER
Lyrics by TIM RICE

Moderately

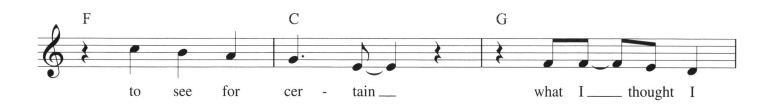

coat with gol - den lin - ing, ___ bright ___ col - ors shin - ing, ___ won - der - ful and new. And in the east ___ ___ the dawn was break - ing, ___ but the world was ___ wak - ing. An - y dream will do. A crash of drums, ___ a flash of light, ___ my ___ gol - den coat flew out of sight. ___ The col - ors fad - ed in - to dark - ness, I was left a - lone. ___ May I re - turn ___

to the ___ be - gin - ning, ___

the light ___ is dim - ming, ___ and the dream is

too. The world ___ and I, ___

we are ___ still wait - ing,

still ___ hes - i - tat - ing. ___ An - y dream will

do. Give me ___ my col - ored coat, my a -

maz - ing col - ored coat. ___ Give me ___ my

Freely

col - ored coat, my a - maz - ing col - ored coat.

Bring Him Home

from LES MISÉRABLES

Music and Lyrics by CLAUDE-MICHEL SCHÖNBERG and ALAIN BOUBLIL
English Lyrics by HERBERT KRETZMER

Slowly, freely

God on

Moderately slow

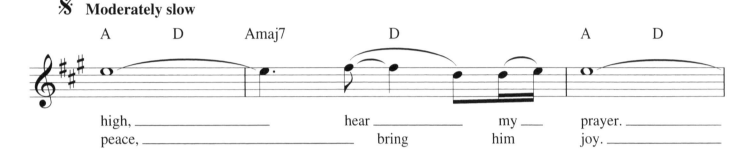

high, _____ hear _____ my _____ prayer. _____
peace, _____ bring him joy. _____

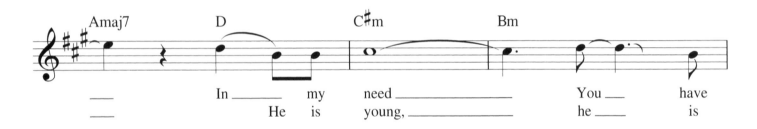

_____ In _____ my need _____ You _____ have
_____ He is young, _____ he _____ is

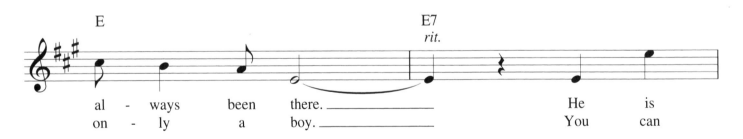

al - ways been there. _____ He is
on - ly a boy. _____ You can

A tempo

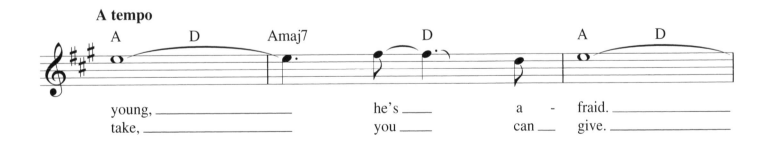

young, _____ he's _____ a - fraid. _____
take, _____ you _____ can _____ give. _____

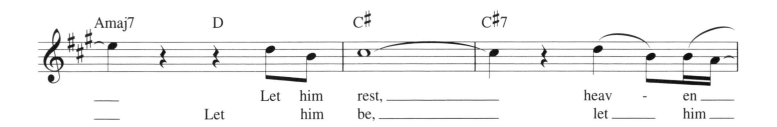

Let him rest, _____ heav - en _____
Let him be, _____ let _____ him _____

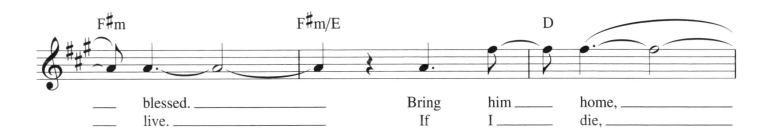

_____ blessed. _____ Bring him _____ home, _____
_____ live. _____ If I _____ die, _____

To Coda ⊕

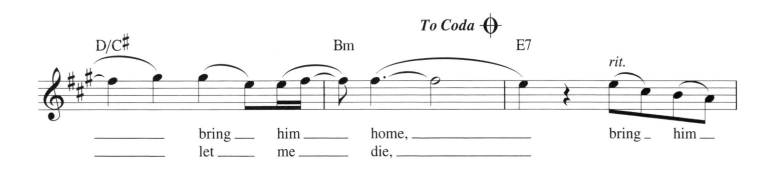

_____ bring _____ him _____ home, _____ bring _____ him _____
_____ let _____ me _____ die, _____

A tempo

home. He's like the son I might have _____ known _____

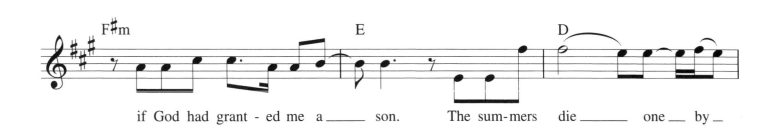

if God had grant - ed me a _____ son. The sum - mers die _____ one _____ by _____

9

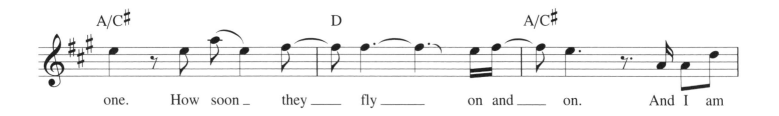

one. How soon _ they ____ fly _____ on and ____ on. And I am

D.S. al Coda

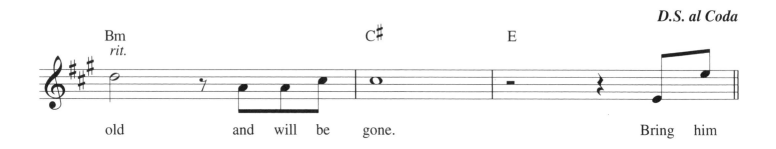

old ____ and will be gone. Bring him

⊕ **Coda** **A tempo**

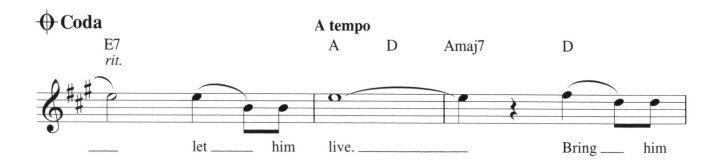

____ let _____ him live. _____ Bring ___ him

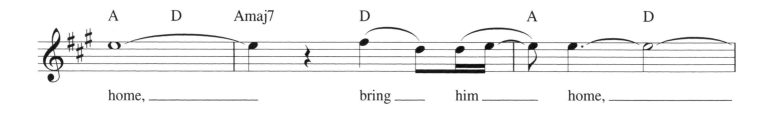

home, _____ bring _____ him _____ home, _____

A tempo

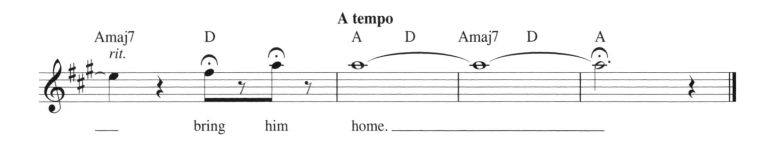

___ bring him home. _____

Elaborate Lives

from Walt Disney Theatrical Productions' AIDA

Music by ELTON JOHN
Lyrics by TIM RICE

14

Seasons of Love

from RENT

Words and Music by JONATHAN LARSON

Moderately

Five hun-dred twen-ty five thou-sand six hun-dred min - utes,

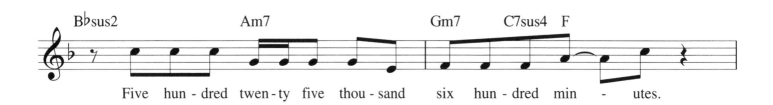

five hun-dred twen-ty five thou-sand mo-ments so ___ dear. ___

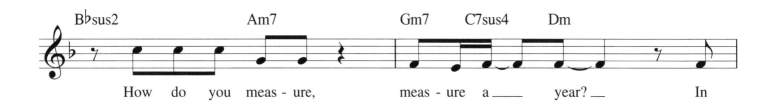

Five hun-dred twen-ty five thou-sand six hun-dred min - utes.

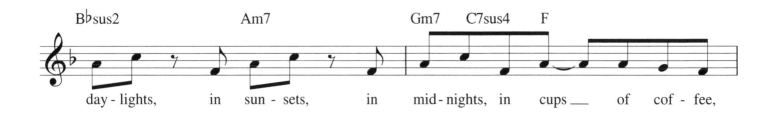

How do you meas-ure, meas-ure a ___ year? ___ In

day-lights, in sun-sets, in mid-nights, in cups ___ of cof-fee,

love. _____

Five hun-dred twen-ty five thou - sand six hun-dred min - utes,

five hun-dred twen-ty five thou - sand jour - neys to __ plan. _____

Five hun-dred twen-ty five thou-sand six hun-dred min - utes. _ How

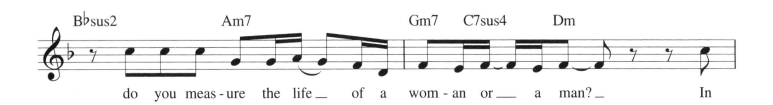

do you meas-ure the life _ of a wom-an or __ a man? _ In

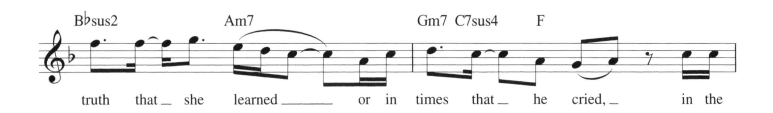

truth that _ she learned _____ or in times that _ he cried, _ in the

bridg - es __ he burned __ or the way that she died. _ It's

time now to sing out, though the sto-ry nev - er ends. _____ Let's

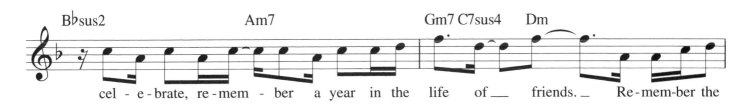

cel - e -brate, re - mem - ber a year in the life of __ friends. _ Re -mem-ber the

love, _____ re -mem-ber the

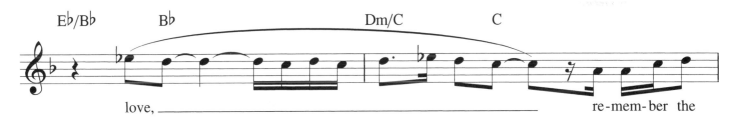

love, _____ re -mem-ber the

love, _____ meas-ure in

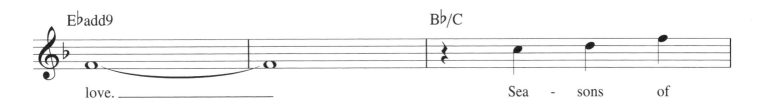

love. _____ Sea - sons of

love, _____ sea -sons of

love. _____

They Live in You

Disney Presents THE LION KING: THE BROADWAY MUSICAL

Music and Lyrics by MARK MANCINA,
JAY RIFKIN and LEBO M

Spiritually, steadily

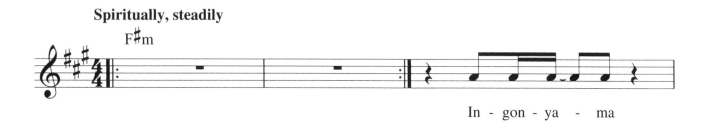

In - gon - ya - ma

nengw' en - a - ma - ba - la.   In - gon - ya - ma

nengw' en - a - ma - ba - la.   Night

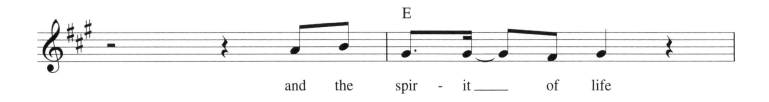

and   the   spir - it _____ of   life

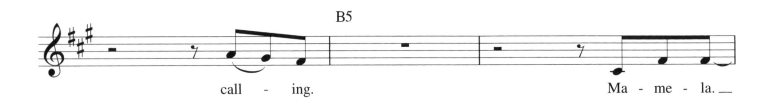

call - ing.   Ma - me - la. _____

_____   And   a   voice

They live in you.   They live _____ in

me.   They're watch - ing   o - ver.

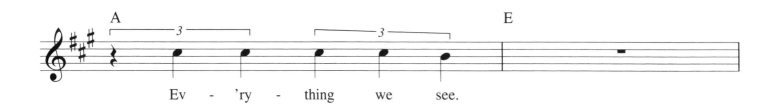

Ev - 'ry - thing we   see.

In ev - 'ry crea - ture.   In   ev - 'ry star. _

_____   In your _ re - flec - tion.

They live _____ in you.

They live   in you. _____

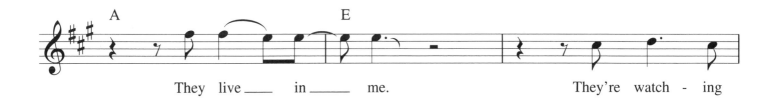

They live ___ in ___ me.   They're watch - ing

o - ver.   Ev - 'ry - thing we see. ___

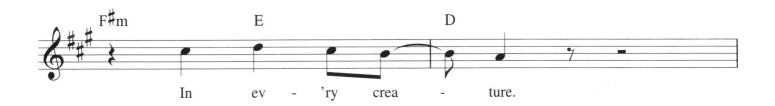

In ev - 'ry crea - ture.

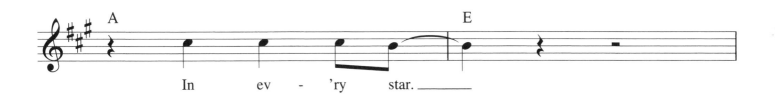

In ev - 'ry star. ___

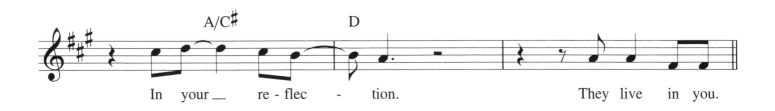

In your ___ re - flec - tion.   They live in you.

In - gon - ya - ma   nengw' en - a - ma - ba - la.

Repeat and fade

In - gon - ya - ma   nengw' en - a - ma - ba - la.

This Is the Moment

from JEKYLL & HYDE

Words by LESLIE BRICUSSE
Music by FRANK WILDHORN

Slowly

This is the mo - ment, this is the

day, when I send all my doubts and de - mons on

their way. ___ Ev - 'ry en - deav - our I ___ have

made ev - er ___ is ___ com - ing in - to play, is

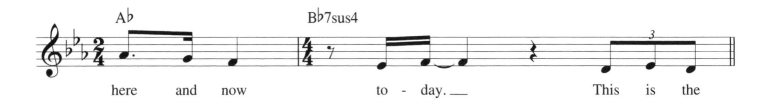

here and now to - day. ___ This is the

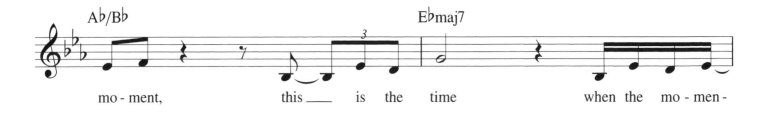

mo - ment, this ___ is the time when the mo - men-

- tum and the mo - ment are __ in __ rhyme. __ Give me this __

__ mo - ment, this __ pre - cious __ chance. __ I'll __

__ gath - er up my past and make some sense __

__ at __ last. __ This is the

mo - ment when all I've __ done, __ all of the

dream - ing, schem - ing and __ scream - ing be - come __ one. __ This is the

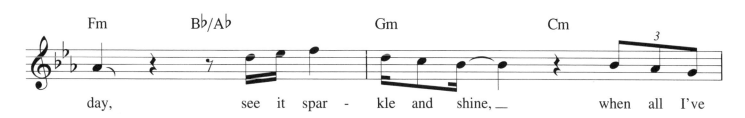

day, see it spar - kle and shine, __ when all I've

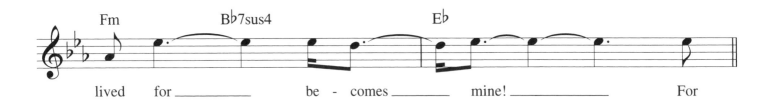

lived for _____ be - comes _____ mine! _____ For

all these ____ years I've faced the world __ a - lone,

and now the time has come to prove to them I made it on

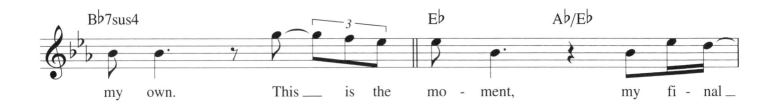

my own. This __ is the mo - ment, my fi - nal __

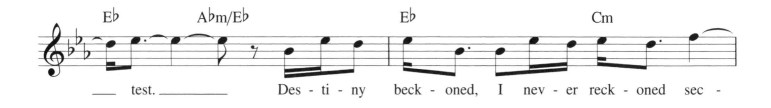

____ test. _____ Des - ti - ny beck - oned, I nev - er reck - oned sec -

- cond __ best. _____ I ___ won't look down, I _____ must not

fall. This is the mo - ment, the sweet - est

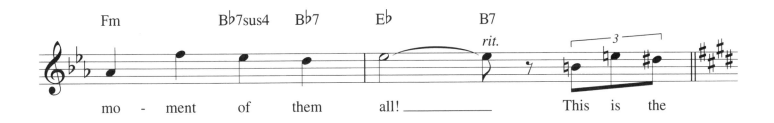

mo - ment of them all! _____ This is the

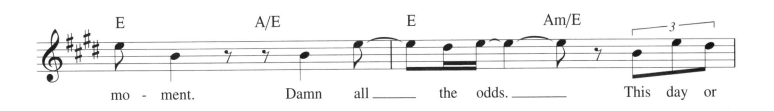

mo - ment. Damn all _____ the odds. _____ This day or

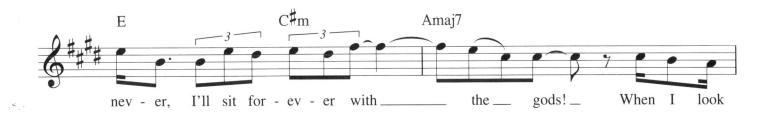

nev - er, I'll sit for - ev - er with _____ the __ gods! _ When I look

back, I will al - ways _ re - call mo - ment for

mo - ment, this _ was the mo - ment, _____ the great - est

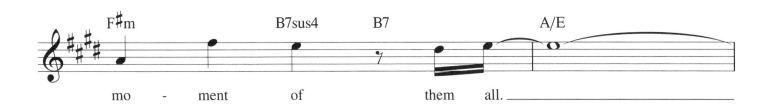

mo - ment of them all. _____

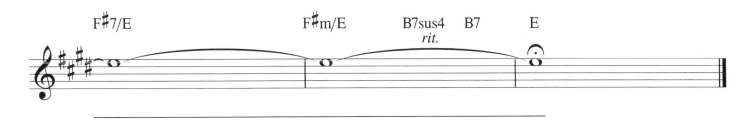

Why God Why?

from MISS SAIGON

Music and Lyrics by CLAUDE-MICHEL SCHÖNBERG,
ALAIN BOUBLIL and RICHARD MALTBY JR.

A tempo

Faster

Cm6/E♭ E♭maj7   G♭/D♭ D♭   G♭/D♭ D♭   A♭/G♭ G♭   A♭/G♭ G♭

A♭ G♭/A♭   A♭   G♭/A♭ A♭   D♭

When I went home be - fore __

D♭maj7   D♭6

__ no one talked of the war. __ What they knew from T.

D♭+   Fm

V. did - n't have a thing to do with me. ___

                                              D♭

I went back and re - upped. __

D♭maj7   D♭6

__ Sure Sai - gon is cor - rupt. __ It felt bet - ter to be __

D♭+   B♭7

__ here driv - ing for the Em - bas - sy. __

E♭m11

'Cause here __ if you can pull a string